THE MEGA GLUTEN-FREE COOKBOOK FOR THE SMART

Quick And Easy Recipes You Will Enjoy

DIANA WATSON

Copyright © 2017 Author Name
All rights reserved.

Table of Contents

Introduction
Chapter 1: Benefits of Going Gluten Free
Chapter 2: Gluten Free Breakfast Recipes
Chapter 3: Gluten Free Lunch Recipes
Chapter 4: Gluten Free Dinner Recipes
Chapter 5: Gluten Free Dessert Recipes
Conclusion

Introduction

Congratulations on purchasing your personal copy of *The Ultimate Gluten Free Cookbook: Healthy and Delicious Recipes for You and Your Loved Ones.* Thank you so much for doing so!

The following chapters will discuss the benefits that a gluten-free lifestyle will provide for you and your family! You will find that the way we typically eat puts out bodies, especially out guts, through a whirlwind of troubles each and every day. If you are tired of feeling bloated and not properly fueled by what you put in your body, this book is a great start to getting yourself to incorporate gluten-free dishes into your everyday life without sacrificing taste!

You will discover how important 'going gluten-free' can be for you and your loved ones, as you see for yourself just how simple it really can be! The information and recipes packed within the contents of this cookbook are a perfect way to get you on the right track to aid your gut in feeling much better! Why live with that wrenching pain from out insides when we can give our bodies proper nourishment by eating more like the way our ancestors did? It is a no-brainer in the long run! A gluten free lifestyle equals feeling healthier and becoming a much more motivated individual!

There are plenty of books on gluten-free eating on the market, thanks again for choosing this one! Every effort was made to ensure it is full of as much useful information as possible. Please enjoy!
Benefits of Going Gluten Free

For those that are unsure on making the decisions to incorporate the gluten free diet in their everyday lifestyle, I hope that by the end of this chapter you will be able to make a clear-cut decision for you and your family!

What *is* gluten? It is a protein that is found commonly in foods like wheat and grains. Gluten's main purpose is to keep the elasticity of foods together during the fermentation process of production. Gluten is the component responsible for making your bread chewy and prevents other edibles from becoming doughy in texture.

The gluten free lifestyle didn't always use to be the craze it is today. There are many individuals our there that have no choice but to cut out foods that contain gluten, for they are quite allergic to this food component and reeks havoc on their bodies if digested. Ailments such as celiac disease, autoimmune digestive disorder, and inflammatory disease are what first initiated the idea of the gluten free lifestyle. Insides the bodies of individuals who suffer from these and other gluten-related diseases, the immune system views gluten as something it needs to attack. The nutrients from gluten-filled edibles are then not absorbed into the body, which in the long run can cause permanent damage and result in major loss of nutrition. People who suffered from these kinds of diseases and even those that just have certain sensitivities to gluten have been ridding their lives of foods filled or made by gluten for years. It didn't use to be as easy to do this, for there were not near as many gluten-free products to utilize out on the market as there is today.

So, what are the benefits of removing gluten from your everyday eating habits?

- **There are limitless alternatives for foods**

that you already consume – Even though items such as flour are out of the question when it comes to gluten-free foods, there are even better and healthier alternatives available to you to utilize, such as rice and quinoa. Nowadays, the possibilities are pretty boundless when it comes to finding foods that are gluten-free. And for those that love to bake and use flour in other dishes, there IS gluten free flour!

- **More energy** – Even though it doesn't sound harmful, when you pair foods filled or produced with gluten with healthier dietary items, you are losing essential vitamins and minerals that your body needs to thrive. Gluten actually can cause more malnutrition than good, for it lacks vitamins that are essential in boosting your energy levels. It has been reported that for those that decide to switch to a gluten-free lifestyle, they no longer need to consume near as much caffeine as they once did before making the switch!

- **Easier digestion** – We all know and recognize those gut wrenching pains and aches that come with digesting our usual foods. For those that do not incorporate gluten in their diets, the actual process of digestion is MUCH easier on the body! Consuming foods that contain no gluten eliminate those pesky tummy aches, extra gas, stomach bloating, cramps, and potential for diarrhea. Right there is a great reason to cut gluten out of your everyday diet if I do not say so myself!

- **Easier time losing unwanted weight** –

Gluten is commonly found in pre-packaged goods, barley, rye, and wheat. Which, most of these edibles are pretty healthy and we are encouraged constantly to fuel our bodies with them. Another great reason to cut out gluten is the fact that it is a component responsible in harboring all that weight that you may have packed on during the winter months or during the holidays. By avoiding foods containing gluten, you are also keeping those not so nutritious options out of your diet that can assist in packing on extra, unwanted pounds. There are LOTS of delicious gluten free alternatives to your favorite foods that are not full of so much extra sugar and unnecessary starches that you can make your new guilty edible pleasures, all the while losing weight! It is a win-win!

- **Lots of vitamins and antioxidants to be found** – When you remove gluten filled foods from your life, you leave much more room to fuel your body with foods that are instead rich in essential vitamins and antioxidants! Obviously, the health benefits of eating more fruits and veggies are pretty endless when you cut out those potato chips and snack bars from your diet. This benefit alone will keep you living a much healthier lifestyle, for food enriched with antioxidants helps fuel a strong immune system, which helps in fighting off sickness throughout the year! Both your physician and wallet will thank you for having to visit your doctor's office much less!

- While there are plenty of great benefits that come with switching over to a gluten free diet of a lifestyle containing less gluten, you still have the responsibility of eating a balanced diet. IF you take the time to read food labels, many edibles that are gluten free can tend to be high in carbohydrates, calories and fat, which all result in weight gain if you are not careful. But, many who have heavily incorporated gluten free foods within their everyday diet have said that they feel more energized and spend less time with the good ol' bathroom throne, which of course gives one much more time to do more productive things.

- If you are still unsure whether going gluten-free is the approach for you, then flip through some of the recipes that fill the remainder of this cookbook! I assure you that you will want to try at least one or two! Even if you are not one to go rogue and throw all your gluten filled edibles in the trash and start from scratch, making and consuming some or all of these recipes will assist you in feeling better!

Gluten Free Breakfast Recipes

Orange Cranberry Scones

What's in it:

- ½ c. dried cranberries
- 1 tsp. vanilla extract
- ¼ c. orange juice
- 2 eggs
- ¼ c. cold 0% fat Greek yogurt
- ¼ c. cold butter
- ½ tsp. salt
- Zest of 1 orange
- 1 tsp. baking powder
- ¼ c. coconut palm sugar
- 1 ¾ c. gluten-free flour
- ¼ c. gluten-free flour (for sprinkling)

How it's made:

- Ensure oven is preheated to 400 degrees
- Mix the dry ingredients together.
- Add butter and Greek yogurt to mixture using either hands or pastry cutter to combine until crumbly in texture.
- Combine vanilla, orange juice, and eggs in a separate bowl
- Mix together wet and dry ingredients until thoroughly combined

- Mix in cranberries
- Shape dough into ball shapes, dropping onto a well-floured surface. Proceed to roll out dough ball into a 1-inch thick circle. Add flour if dough starts to become too sticky.
- Cut circle into quarters and then cut those quarters in half, creating 8 scones.
- Place scones on lined baking sheet
- Bake for 15-20 minutes
- Let cool and add icing if desired before serving
-
- **Two Ingredient Pancakes**
-
- **What's in it:**
-
- 2 eggs
- 1 super ripe banana, mashed
- (Coconut oil, for pan)
-
- **How it's made:**
-
- Mash ripe banana with fork
- Whisk eggs in a separate bowl, proceed to mix eggs and banana together
- Pour coconut oil in a pan over low-medium heat.
- Pour enough batter in pan to make a silver dollar shaped pancake
- Let cake sit in pan for 30 seconds on each side
- Pair with fresh berries and a dollop of whipped cream or syrup. Enjoy!

Gluten-Free Lunch Recipes

Five-Spice Turkey and Lettuce Wraps

What's in it:

- 1 shredded carrot
- ½ c. fresh herbs (chives, basil, mint, cilantro, etc)
- ½ tsp. salt
- 1 tsp. five-spice powder
- 2 tbsp. hoisin sauce
- ½ c. reduced sodium chicken broth
- 1 8 oz. can water chestnuts
- 1 red bell pepper
- 1 tbsp. fresh ginger
- 1 pound lean ground turkey
- 2 tsp. sesame oil
- ½ c. water
- ½ c. instant brown rice
- 2 heads lettuce

How it's made:

- In a saucepan, boil rice
- While rice cooks, in a large pan heat oil and proceed with turkey and ginger. Cooking until crumbled and cooked through.
- Mix in rice, pepper, chestnuts, broth, hoisin, five-spice and salt. Cook until entirely heated through
- Divide lettuce leaves, then spoon turkey

mixture into leaves
- Top turkey leaves with carrot and herbs, and then roll up into wraps
-
- **Curried Squash and Chicken Soup**
-
- **What's in it:**
-
- ¼ tsp. salt
- ½-1 tsp. Thai red curry paste
- 2 tsp. brown sugar
- 2 tsp. lime juice
- 1 6 oz. bag baby spinach
- 8 oz. boneless/skinless chicken breast
- ½ c. water
- ½ c. coconut milk
- 1 10 oz. package frozen pureed winter squash
-
- **How it's made:**
-
- In a pan over medium-high heat, heat water, coconut milk and squash. Ensure to stir occasionally. Heat until squash is totally defrosted.
- Pour in chicken and reduce heat to just a simmer
- Mix in salt, paste, sugar, lime juice and spinach and cook until chicken is thoroughly cooked
-
-

Gluten-Free Dinner Recipes

Lasagna-Stuffed Spaghetti Squash

What's in it:

- 3 oz. part-skim mozzarella
- ¾ c. marinara
- 8 oz. frozen broccoli florets
- Salt and pepper
- ¼ c. Romano cheese
- 1 c. small curd cottage cheese
- 2 spaghetti squash

How it's made:

- Split the squash and then remove the seeds.
- Place squash in microwave on parchment for 9-11 minutes on high
- While squash is tenderizing, preheat broiler
- Mix together cottage cheese, pepper, and Romano. Then fold in broccoli
- Season squash with salt and pepper. Scrape up squash strands with a fork, leaving them in squash.
- Divide cheese mixture evenly among halves and top with sauce and mozzarella cheese. Broil until the filling is heated.
- Serve alongside salad if desired

Honey Salmon with Quinoa Salad

What's in it:

- ½ tsp. cayenne pepper
- 1 ¼ pound skinless salmon
- 12 oz. cabbage
- Salt and pepper
- 2 tbsp. + 2 tsp. honey
- 1 tbsp. ginger
- 2 tbsp. oil
- 2 lines
- 2 scallions
- 1 c. quinoa

How it's made:

- In a pan cook quinoa until toasted. Add 2 cups of water and cover. Let sit over very low heat for around ten minutes. After, take the dish off of the heat and allow to stand for 5 minutes. Fluff with fork.
- Slice scallions, grate 1 lime and squeeze juice from lime. Mix oil, honey, ginger, 2 teaspoons honey and ¼ teaspoon of salt and pepper. Mix in scallion (both parts, except darkest portion) and toss with cabbage.
- Line a baking sheet with foil, preheat broiler
- Place salmon on pan, sprinkling with cayenne pepper, salt, and remainder of honey. Broil until browned on top
- Fold in quinoa into cabbage mixture then sprinkle with dark portion of scallions. Serve alongside salmon, with a wedge of lime.

Gluten-Free Dessert Recipes

Flourless Chocolate Cake

What's in it:

- ¼ c. confectioners' sugar + extra for dusting
- ½ c. sour cream
- 1 ¼ c. heavy cream
- 1 c. granulated sugar
- 5 eggs
- 8 oz. bittersweet chocolate, chopped
- ¼ c. unsweetened cocoa powder + extra for pan
- 1 c. unsalted butter

How it's made:

- Ensure oven is preheated to 350 degrees
- Heat butter and ¼ cup heavy cream in pan over medium heat until butter is melted. Add in chocolate and stir until melted and smooth in texture. Remove from heat.
- Mix together cocoa powder, granulated sugar, and eggs, then whisk in chocolate mixture
- Pour in a prepared pan
- Bake for 35-40 minutes until puffed. Let cool for at least 1 hour.
- Run knife around pan and unmold cake
- Beat remaining heavy cream with sour cream and confectioners' sugar until peaks form. Dust cake with cocoa and/or confectioners' and serve along with whipped mixture

Conclusion

You have made it to the end of *The Ultimate Gluten Free Cookbook: Healthy and Delicious Recipes for You and Your Loved Ones.* I hope the contents of this book helped you to realize how beneficial as well as simple it is to incorporate the gluten free lifestyle right into your everyday life.

The chapters of this book should be a great roadmap to get you headed down the path to feeling better. Trust me, your gut will be thanking you in the near future and hopefully years to come! You have the tools necessary to kickstart your goal of getting you and your family hooked on a gluten-free diet TODAY. What are you waiting for?

The next step is to take the information and delicious recipes within this book and put them to the test upon the family dinner table. You will be surprised just how tasteful gluten free recipes can be! Your taste buds will not be missing out, but rather your body will be getting rid of all that unnecessary stuff we pack our bodies with on a daily basis without even realizing it. Our bodies are our temples; shouldn't we be treating them and fueling them as such?

Finally, I will leave you with a big GOOD LUCK as you venture into the ways of a gluten free life. You will not regret your decision!

BOOK TWO
INSULIN

RESISTANCE DIET PLAN FOR TYPE 2 DIABETICS

YOUR ESSENTIAL GUIDE TO DIABETES PREVENTION AND DELICIOUS RECIPES YOU CAN ENJOY!

DIANA WATSON

TABLE OF CONTENTS

- THE MEGA GLUTEN-FREE COOKBOOK FOR THE SMART
- INTRODUCTION
- UNDERSTAND THE RESISTANCE
- INSULIN RESISTANCE DIET
- LONG-TERM MANAGEMENT
- DIET PLAN
- RECIPES

- **VIP Subscriber List**
- Hi Dear Reader, this is Diana! If you like my book and you want to receive the latest tips and tricks on cooking, weight-loss, cookbook recipes and more, do <u>subscribe to my mailing list in the link here</u>! I will then be able to send you the most up-to-date information about my upcoming books and promotions as well! <u>Thank you for supporting my work and happy reading!</u>
- INTRODUCTION
- Congratulations on purchasing your personal copy of *Insulin Resistance Diet Plan for Type 2 Diabetics.* Thank you for doing so.
- If you find you are being warned by your doctor that you are at high risk of developing diabetes, or that you have insulin resistance, you're not alone. In fact, it's believed that the number of diabetics is going to double from

around 190 million to 325 million within the next couple of decades. A study performed in 2002 found that 32.2% of the population in the US are insulin resistant.

- Knowing how insulin resistance works on a cellular level helps people know the best ways to treat and prevent type 2 diabetes. Individuals who suffer from diabetes mellitus and obese people are often insulin resistant. Many studies have discovered that an insulin resistance diet and exercise can alter the pathways and slow down the onset of insulin resistance.

- It's safe to say that if we look at ways to change our habits, and pay attention to what we do, we can make some improvements to our life. An insulin resistance diet can help you to lose weight and will turn regulate your blood glucose and insulin levels so that your chances of developing diabetes are lowered.

- It's possible that insulin resistance is the leading cause of many of today's chronic diseases. These diseases are collectively killing over a million people each year. The good thing is that it can easily be improved with some simple changed in your eating, lifestyle, and exercise habits. Preventing the chance of insulin resistance is probably the best thing you can do to make sure you live a long, healthy life.
- There are plenty of books on this subject on the market, thanks again for choosing this one! Every effort was made to ensure it is full of as much useful information as possible. Please enjoy!
- Congratulations on downloading your personal copy of *Insulin Resistance Diet Plan for Type 2 Diabetics*. Thank you for doing so.

- UNDERSTAND THE RESISTANCE
- There are times when our cells quit responding to our insulin. When this happens, you are likely suffering from insulin resistance. Your cells become resistant to insulin. When your body becomes resistant, your pancreas will respond by producing more insulin to try and reduce your blood sugar levels. When this happens you develop hyperinsulinemia, which is when the blood contains high levels of insulin. Let's make this a little easier, let's look at the separate parts of insulin resistance.

- **Metabolism**

- Metabolism is probably one of the most misunderstood processes that the body goes through. Your metabolism works as a collection of chemical reactions that happens in your cells to help you convert food into energy. As you are reading this, a thousand metabolic reactions are happening. There are two main metabolic channels.

- Catabolism is the process your body goes through when breaking down you food components, as in fats, proteins, and carbs, into simpler parts, which are then used for energy. To better understand it, look at it as if it is your destructive metabolism. Your cells break down fats and carbs to release their energy; this ensures that your body can fuel an anabolic reaction.

- Anabolism is the contrastive metabolism which works to build and store energy. When your cells perform an anabolic process, it helps to grow new cells and to maintain your body tissues, and it also helps to store energy that you can use later.

- The nervous and hormone systems control these processes. When you look at how many calories you should consume in a day, you have to check your body's total energy expenditure. What you eat, how much you move, how you rest, and how well your tissues and cells recuperate will all go into figuring out your total energy expenditure.

- Your metabolism is made up of three main components:

1. Basal metabolic rate – this how many calories you body can burn while at rest, and also contributes to 50 to 80 percent of the amount of energy you body uses.

2. How much energy is used during activity – this is how many calories your body burns when you are active. This takes up 20% of your total expenditure.

3. Warming effects of your food – this is how many calories you use when you eat, digest,

and metabolize your food.

4. Insulin

5. Insulin is a hormone that the pancreas produces and releases into your blood. Insulin help to keep your blood sugar at a reasonable level by promoting cell growth and division, protein and lipid metabolism, regulating carbohydrates, and glucose uptake. Insulin helps your cells absorb glucose to use for energy.

6. After you eat, and your blood sugar levels rise, insulin is released. The glucose and insulin travel throughout your blood to your cells. It helps to stimulate the muscle tissue and liver; helps liver, fat, and muscle cells to absorb glucose; and lowers glucose levels by reducing the glucose production in your liver.

7. People who suffer from type 1 or type 2

diabetes may have to take insulin shot to help their bodies metabolize glucose correctly. Type 1 diabetic's pancreas doesn't make insulin, and the beta cells have been destroyed. There's typically no chance of preventing type 1, and most of the time a person is born with it. Type 2 diabetic's pancreas still make insulin, but the body doesn't respond to it.

8. Symptoms

9. If you go to the doctor, they will likely test your fasting insulin levels. If you have high levels, then chances are you are insulin resistant. You can also do an oral glucose tolerance test. This is where you will be given a dose of glucose, and they will check your blood sugar levels for the next few hours.

10. People who are obese or overweight, and

people with a lot of fat in the mid-section, are at a greater risk of being insulin resistant. Acanthosis nigrans, a skin condition characterized by dark spots on the skin, can be a symptom of insulin resistance. Also, if you have low HDL and high triglycerides, then your chances are higher as well.

11. For the most part, insulin resistance and pre-diabetes have no significant symptoms. They main way to find out if you have either one is to get tested by your doctor. Now, you're probably wondering how to know if you should be tested. Here are some reasons why you should:

- Body Mass Index over 25
- Over age 45
- Have CVD
- Physically inactive

- Parent or sibling with diabetes

- Family background of Pacific Islander American, Hispanic/Latino, Asian American, Native American, Alaska Native, or African American

- Had a baby that weighed more than 9 pounds

- Diagnoses of gestational diabetes

- High blood pressure – 140/90 or higher

- HDL below 35 or triglyceride above 250

- Have polycystic ovary syndrome

- If your tests come back as normal, be sure to be retested every three years, at least. But, you don't have to wait until you get positive test results to start changing your life. In fact, if you have any of the risk factors, even if it's just a family history, you start changing now, and you may never have to hear that diagnoses.

-
- INSULIN RESISTANCE DIET
- Years of research has found that excess weight is the primary cause of insulin resistance. This means that weight loss can help you body better respond to insulin. Studies performed by the Diabetes Prevention Program have found that people who are pre-diabetic and insulin resistance can prevent or slow down the development of diabetes by fixing their diet.

- **Guidelines**

- Here are the main seven ways you go start to develop an insulin resistance diet:

1. Reduce Carbohydrate Intake

2. Studies that have been published in *Diabetes, Metabolic Syndrome and Obesity* suggest that controlling the number of carbohydrates you

eat is essential in controlling your glycemic index. You can count all carbs you eat, but it's best if you make sure you consume your carbs from dairy products, legumes, whole grains, fruits, and veggies.

3. Stay Away From Sweetened Beverages

4. All sugars will raise your blood sugar levels, but the American Diabetes Association has now advised, specifically, to avoid sugar-sweetened drinks. This includes iced tea, fruit drinks, soft drinks, and vitamin or energy water drinks that have artificial sweeteners, concentrates, high fructose corn syrup, or sucrose.

5. Consume More Fiber

6. Glycemia is improved in people who consume more than 50 grams of fiber each day. Large prospective cohort studies have shown that

whole grain consumption is associated with a lower risk of type 2 diabetes.

7. Consume Healthy Fats

8. Studies have shown that fatty acids are more important than total fat. People who suffer from insulin resistance should consume unsaturated fats instead of trans fatty acids or saturated fats.

9. Consume Plenty of Protein

10. *International Journal of Vitamin and Nutrition Research* published a study in 2011 that discovered people who were on a diet to treat obesity had better results when they consumed more protein.

11. Consume Dairy

12. More and more studies are finding that dairy consumption is linked to a reduced risk of type 2 diabetes.

13. Watch Your Portions

14. Losing weight is key in reducing your risk for diabetes. One great way to do that controls your portion sizes. It's best to eat more small meals instead of three large meals.

15. Bad Foods

16. When you start the insulin resistance diet, there are certain foods that you need to avoid, or at least reduce your intake of. Here are some of the foods that you need to watch out for.

- Red meat – contains lots of saturated fats that can exacerbate the problems

- Certain cheeses – cheese that is high in fat will cause more problems

- Fried food – this is a bad dietary choice no matter what diet you're on

- Grains – processed or refined carbs can lead

higher insulin levels

- Potatoes – these foods turn into sugar in your system

- Pumpkin – these are just like potatoes

- Carrots – these aren't entirely bad for you, just limit your intake because they are high in sugar

- Doughnuts – these are full insulin raising ingredients

- Alcohol – these turn straight to sugar when you drink them

- **Good Foods**

- Now that you know the main foods you should stay away from, here are the foods you should consume.

- Broccoli, Spinach, Collard greens – these, as well as most other leafy greens, are a great source of magnesium, zinc, vitamin E, C, and A

- Broccoli sprouts
- Swiss Chard, Romaine Lettuce, Arugula, Green Cabbage, and Kale – these also contain high amounts of nutrients
- Blueberries – contain anthocyanins which simulate the release of adiponectin which helps regular blood sugar
- Indian gooseberry – these can regulate blood sugar and reduce hyperglycemia
- Walnuts – any nut is great food for an insulin resistance diet
- These are just a few of some of the foods you should consume. Many other foods have the same properties as the ones on this list, as well as a few other types of benefits.
-
-

-
- LONG-TERM MANAGEMENT
- Once you have started a diet, the hardest thing is sticking with it. The good thing about this diet is that it isn't anything drastic, and you can quickly change your diet with a few tweaks. To ensure that you have lasting results, let's look at some of the best ways to maintain.
- Be sure to keep up regular exercise. Exercise can help lower your blood sugar, reduce body fat, and help you lose weight. Your cells will also become more insulin sensitive as well. You don't have to do anything spectacular either. Any movement will help you; gardening, running, swimming, walking, or dancing all count for exercise.
- Remember that weight loss isn't going to be linear. You may start dropping pounds when you first start, but you will eventually hit a

plateau. You have to be proactive with your diet. When you notice you are hitting a plateau, start to make little changes to push past it.

- Try to pay attention to when you eat. If you notice that you eat when you are stress, upset, sad, bored, lonely, or low on energy take note of it. Look for other ways to move past those emotions to prevent emotional eating.
- Find some cheerleaders. I don't mean paying people to follow you around all day cheering, that would get annoying. I mean you should find a support system. The main reason why diet programs like Jenny Craig and Weight Watchers works are because of the meeting and people to talk to. There's no need to pay big bucks for this thought. You can get your family and friends to help you out, and you can probably find a Facebook group to help you

out.

- **Side Effects**
- With any diet, you will experience some side effects. These side effects will either be longer-term or short-term. Let's look at some side effects that you may experience when you begin the insulin resistance diet.
- Short-term:
    - Cravings – this is normal when you start to change your diet. Your body becomes freaked out when you start to eat healthier foods and reduce the snack foods that you're used to eating. Keep reminding yourself why you're doing this. The cravings will eventually pass.
    - Headaches – this is because your body has become addicted to the processed foods you're used to eating. You're going to withdrawals. Once you get all the bad

food out of your system, the headaches will stop.

- o Lower energy – this is another symptom you will have because of withdrawals. Your energy levels will drop. Your body is doing a lot of work when you start eating healthier, so be patient with it.

- Long-term:

    - o Weight loss – this is probably the best thing that will happen to you on this diet. Weight loss will help to improve all of your health problems.

    - o Less hunger and cravings – you may start out having more cravings, but once that phase passes, you won't be bothered with the hunger and cravings like you used to be.

    - o Lower blood pressure – a diet that is low

in sugar and trans and saturated fats, your blood pressure will lower. This reduces your risk of heart disease, heart attack, stroke, and several other health problems.

- More energy – getting rid of high glycemic index foods will give bursts of energy that you have never had. Plus, you will no longer have the rollercoaster effect from your blood sugar highs and lows.
- Better mood and concentration – with your old diet, you probably had mood boosts followed by a sudden plummet. With the insulin resistance diet, you will keep a more steady mood and concentration throughout the day.
- Better immune system – since you won't be consuming as many inflammatory and

allergenic foods you will be able to improve your overall immune system and health.

- Increased digestion – with this diet you will reduce your intake of sugar, dairy, and gluten. These foods are the most common foods to cause digestive problems. Since you won't be consuming as many of these foods, your digestive system will work better. You will also increase your fiber intake, so this will aid your gastrointestinal tract as well.
- As you can see, the long-term side effects are better than the short-term side effects; there are also more long-term effects. It's easy to see the good outweighs the bad. It's a no brainer that this is an easy and simple diet to follow.
-

-
- DIET PLAN
- To help get you started, here is a 5-day meal plan. All of the recipes will follow in the next chapter.
- <u>Day One</u>
- Breakfast: Basil and Tomato Frittata
- Frittatas are the perfect breakfast to help use up leftovers. Pair this with a slice of whole grain toast and fruit.
- Lunch: Carrot and Butternut Squash Soup
- You'll never go back to canned soups after you try this.
- Dinner: Grilled Shrimp Skewers
- This is a quick meal because shrimp only takes a few minutes to cook.
- <u>Day Two</u>

- Breakfast: Pecan, Carrot, and Banana Muffins
- This is a meal you can serve to your friends, and nobody will ever know that they are healthy. It's the perfect guilt-free treat.
- Lunch: Lemony Hummus
- Creating your hummus is a great meal. You have control over its flavor and salt levels.
- Dinner: Chicken Tortilla Soup
- This is perfect if you have some leftover chicken. This spicy soup will satisfy everyone.
- <u>Day Three</u>
- Breakfast: Dried Fruit, Seeds, and Nuts Granola

- This is great to mix up a large amount on the weekend and portion it out for the following week.
- There is a high carb content because of the dried fruit, but you can easily fix that by reducing the fruit or leaving it out entirely.
- Lunch: Quinoa Tabbouleh Salad
- Quinoa is the perfect food because not only is it gluten-free, but it's also considered a protein. This is a delicious meal for meat-eaters and vegetarians.
- Dinner: Rice and Beef Stuffed Peppers
- These little peppers look sophisticated, but the entire family will love eating them up.
- <u>Day Four</u>

- Breakfast: Goat Cheese and Veggie Scramble
- This is the perfect savory breakfast. With the onions, tomatoes, peppers, eggs, and cheese you have the perfect well-rounded meal.
- Lunch: Curried Chicken Salad
- The Greek yogurt and mayo adds creaminess to the sandwich that you won't get anywhere else.
- Dinner: Jamaican Pork Tenderloin with Beans
- This is a quick summertime meal that everybody will love. Serve alongside some pilaf or brown rice.
- <u>Day Five</u>
- Breakfast: Superfood Smoothie

- This four ingredient smoothie is quick to whip up and won't run you late.
- Lunch: Tomato and Spinach Pasta
- This dish is perfect for lunch or dinner. Make a double portion so you can have some later in the week.
- Dinner: Grilled Turkey Burgers
- It should never be said that you can't have a tasty and healthy burger. Fix some sweet potato fries to complete this meal.

- RECIPES
- **Sides & Extras**
- **Salsa**
- Ingredients:
- Salt
- 1 tbsp olive oil
- ½ lime
- 1 minced garlic clove
- 1/3 c coriander, chopped
- 1 jalapeno, chopped
- 1 onion, chopped
- 2 tomatoes, chopped
- Instructions:
- Mix everything together. Add salt to your taste. Allow refrigerating for 30 minutes.

-
- **Oven-Roasted Tomatoes**
- Ingredients:
- salt
- 1 tbsp oil
- 4 thyme sprigs
- 1-pint cherry tomatoes, halved
- Instructions:
- The oven should be at 320. Place the tomatoes on a prepared baking sheet. Top with salt and thyme and drizzle with oil. Cook for 45 minutes.
-

-
- **Zucchini Chips**
- Ingredients:
- salt
- 1 tbsp olive oil
- 4 zucchini, sliced
- Instructions:
- Place the zucchini slices on a prepared baking sheet. Top with oil and salt.
- Cook for 30 minutes at 320 until they brown.

-
- **Breakfast**

- **Basil and Tomato Frittata**

- Ingredients:

- ½ c Italian cheese, reduced-fat

- ¼ tsp pepper

- ¼ tsp salt

- 8 egg whites

- ¼ c basil, sliced

- 2 plum tomatoes

- 1 minced garlic clove

- 2 tsp EVOO

- ¼ c onion, chopped

- Instructions:

- Cook the onion in a hot skillet until it has become tender. Mix the garlic until fragrant.

Stir in the tomato and cook until all the liquid is absorbed. Add in the basil.

- Mix the pepper, salt, and eggs. Pour into the skillet over the veggies, and top with cheese. Slide the skillet into an oven that is set to broil. Cook until the eggs are set.

- **Pecan, Carrot, and Banana Muffin**

- Ingredients:

- ¼ c pecans, chopped

- 1 tsp vanilla

- ½ c banana, mashed

- ¾ c carrot, shredded

- 1/3 c yogurt, sugar-free

- 1 egg

- 1/3 c brown sugar

- ¼ c canola oil

- ½ tsp salt

- ¼ tsp baking soda

- 1 tsp cinnamon

- 1 tsp baking powder

- 1 c whole wheat flour

- Instructions:

- Mix the flour, baking powder, cinnamon, baking soda, and salt together.

- Mix all the other ingredients, except for the nuts. Once combine, mix into the flour mixture. Gently fold in the pecans.

- Pour into a prepared 6-cup muffin tin. In should bake for 22 minutes at 375.

- **Homemade Granola**
- Ingredients:
- ½ c brown sugar
- 1 ½ tsp salt
- ¼ c maple syrup
- ¾ c honey
- 1 c oil
- 2 tsp vanilla
- ½ c dried apricots
- ½ c sultans
- ½ c dried cranberries
- ½ c coconut flakes
- 1 c cashews
- 1 c walnuts
- ½ c flaked almonds
- 1 c pecans, chopped
- ½ c pepitas
- 1 c sunflower seeds
- 8 c rolled oats

- Directions:
- The oven should be at 325. Mix the nuts, coconut, and oats. In a pot mix the brown sugar, vanilla, sugar, oil, honey, maple syrup and allow to boil. Let it cook for five minutes until thick. Pour the sugar mixture over the nuts and quickly stir together.
- Place the mixture on baking sheets lined with foil. Cook for 10 minutes. Remove and mix up the mixture. Bake for another 10 minutes. Once it's browned, mix in the dried fruits. Once cool, seal in a bowl or bag.
-

- **Goat Cheese and Veggie Scramble**
- Ingredients:
- ¼ c goat cheese
- ¼ tsp pepper
- ¼ tsp salt
- 1 c egg substitute
- ½ c tomato, chopped
- 2 tsp olive oil
- ¼ c onion, chopped
- ¼ c bell pepper, chopped
- Instructions:
- Cook the pepper and onion until soft. Mix in the tomato and cook until liquid is absorbed. Turn down the heat and add in the egg substitute, pepper, and salt. Scramble the egg until cooked through. Top with goat cheese.

-
- **Superfood Smoothie**
- Instructions:
- 1 banana
- 2 c spinach
- 1 c blueberries, frozen
- 1 c almond milk
- Instructions:
- Place everything in your blender and mix until smooth.

-
- **Lunch**

- **Carrot and Butternut Squash Soup**

- ¼ c half-and-half, fat-free

- ¼ tsp nutmeg

- ¼ tsp pepper

- 2 14 ½ -oz can chicken broth, reduced-sodium

- ¾ c leeks, sliced

- 2 c carrots, sliced

- 3 c butternut squash, diced

- 1 tbsp butter

- Instructions:

- Melt the butter in a large pot. Place the leek, carrot, and squash in the hot pot. Put on the lid, and allow to cook for about eight minutes. Pour in the broth. Allow everything to come to boil. Turn down the heat to a simmer. Place the lid on the pot and let cook for 25 minutes. The veggies should be tender.

- With an immersion blender, mix the soup to the consistency that you like. Season with the nutmeg and the pepper. Bring everything back to a boil and stir in the half-and-half.

-

- **Lemony Hummus**
- Ingredients:
- ¼ c water
- 1 tbsp EVOO
- ¼ tsp cumin
- ¼ tsp pepper
- ½ tsp salt
- 1 clove garlic, chopped
- 1 ½ tbsp tahini
- ¼ c lemon juice
- 15-oz chickpeas, drained
- Directions:
- Add everything except for the water and oil in a food processor. Mix until combine. Add the oil and water and continue mixing until smooth. Add extra water if you need to.

-
- **Quinoa Tabbouleh**
- Ingredients:
- 2 scallions, sliced
- ½ c mint, chopped
- 2/3 c parsley
- 1-pint cherry tomatoes
- 1 large cucumber
- pepper
- ½ c EVOO
- 1 minced garlic clove
- 2 tbsp lemon juice
- ½ tsp salt
- 1 c quinoa, rinsed
- Instructions:
- Cook the quinoa in salted water. As the quinoa cooks, mix the garlic and lemon juice. Slowly

whisk in the EVOO, and then sprinkle with pepper and salt to your taste.

- Allow the quinoa to cool completely. Toss with the dressing and then mix in the remaining ingredients. Add extra pepper and salt if needed.

- **Curried Chicken Salad**
- Ingredients:
- 4 whole wheat pita rounds
- 2 c mixed greens
- 1 c green grapes
- ¼ tsp pepper
- ¼ tsp salt
- 1 tsp curry powder
- 3 tbsp mayo, reduced-fat
- ½ c Greek yogurt, nonfat
- ¼ c slivered almonds
- 1 ¼-lb chicken, shredded
- Instructions:
- Mix all of the ingredients except for the greens and pitas. Divide the chicken mixture into each pita. Top each with some greens.

-
- **Tomato and Spinach Pasta**
- Instructions:
- 3 tbsp parmesan, grated
- 1 tbsp balsamic vinegar
- ¼ tsp pepper
- 2 minced garlic cloves
- 1 c grape tomatoes
- 8 c spinach
- 2 tbsp olive oil
- 8-oz whole-wheat spaghetti
- Instructions:
- Cook the spaghetti the way the package says to, but without the salt. Drain.
- As the pasta cooks, sauté the spinach until it wilts. Stir in the tomatoes and cook for about three minutes. Mix in the garlic.

- Toss the pasta with the veggies and all the other ingredients.

-
- **Dinner**
- **Grilled Shrimp Skewers**
- Ingredients:
- 9 skewers, soaked
- 1 lb cleaned shrimp
- 2 scallions, minced
- ¼ tsp pepper
- ½ tsp salt
- ¼ tsp red pepper flakes
- 1 medium lemon, zest, and juice
- 2 minced garlic cloves
- 1 ½ tbsp olive oil
- Instructions:
- Prepare your grill.
- Mix the scallions, pepper, salt, pepper flakes,

lemon juice and zest, garlic, and oil.

- Place the shrimp in the mixture and coat. Allow to marinate in the refrigerate for 30 minutes.

- Place the shrimp evenly among the skewers. Get rid on any remaining marinade.

- Grill them shrimp until pink and firm, around two to three minutes.

-

- **Chicken Tortilla Soup**
- Ingredients:
- 1 c tortilla chips
- 2 minced garlic cloves
- 1 c chicken broth, reduced-sodium
- 2 c stir-fry veggies
- 2 c chicken, shredded
- 2 ½ c water
- 1 14 ½-oz can stewed tomatoes, Mexican-style
- Directions:
- In a crock pot, mix the garlic, broth, veggies, chicken, water, and tomatoes.
- Cook for six and a half hours on low.
- Top with chips.

- **Rice and Beef Stuffed Peppers**
- Ingredients:
- 1 tbsp parsley, divided
- ½ tsp pepper
- 2 tsp salt
- 4 minced garlic cloves
- ½ c tomato sauce
- ¼ c parsley
- ½ c Parmigiano-Reggiano, shredded
- 1 ½ c rice, cooked
- 1 ½ lb ground beef
- ¼ tsp red pepper flakes
- 1 c beef broth
- ½ onion, sliced
- 2 ½ c tomato sauce
- 6 bell peppers
- Instructions:
- The oven should be at 375. Cut the tops off the peppers and clean out the insides. Poke a few

small holes in the bottom of each.

- Place 2 ½ cups tomato sauce in a casserole dish. Place in the pepper flakes, broth, and onion. Set the peppers upright in the mixture.
- Mix the pepper, salt, garlic, 2 tbsp tomato sauce, ¼ c parsley, cheese, rice, and beef. Divide the mixture between the peppers. Add a tablespoon of tomato sauce on top of each and lay the pepper tops back on. Top dish with parchment paper and then tin foil. Place the dish on a baking sheet.
- Cook for an hour. They should be starting to feel soft. Take off the foil and parchment and cook for an addition 25 minutes.
-

- **Jamaican Pork Tenderloin**
- Ingredients:
- ½ tsp pepper
- ¼ tsp salt
- 1 tbsp lemon juice
- 1 tsp lemon zest
- 1 tbsp EVOO
- 1 lb green beans
- 3 c water
- 2 tbsp Creole mustard
- ¼ c grape jelly
- 2 tsp Jerk seasoning
- ¼ c orange juice, divided
- ¾ lb pork tenderloin
- Instructions:
- Mix the pepper, salt, lemon juice and zest, EVOO and water. Bring everything to a boil and add in the beans.
- As the beans cook, mix the mustard, jelly, jerk

seasoning, and half the orange juice. Cover the tenderloin. The oven should be set and 350. Place the tenderloin in a casserole dish and pour in the rest of the orange juice. Bake for 45 minutes.

-

-
- **Grilled Turkey Burgers**
- Ingredients:
- 4 whole-wheat buns
- ½ tsp curry
- ¼ c Dijon
- 12-oz ground turkey
- 1/8 tsp pepper
- ¼ tsp garlic salt
- ¼ tsp Italian seasoning
- 2 tbsp milk, fat-free
- 2 tbsp bread crumbs
- ¼ c green onions, sliced
- ½ c carrot, shredded
- Instructions:
- Mix the ground turkey with the seasonings, bread crumbs, and veggies. Form the meat mixture into four patties.
- Prepare your grill, and cook the patties until done.

- Mix the mustard and curry powder and spread onto the buns. Add the burgers to the buns. Top with tomato and lettuce if desired.

-

- **Dessert**

- **Blueberries and Yogurt**

- Ingredients:

- 1/3 c Greek yogurt

- 10 blueberries

- Instructions:

- Top the yogurt with the blueberries and enjoy.

-

-
- **Raspberry Sorbet**
- Ingredients:
- lemon juice
- 1 c raspberries
- Instructions:
- Place the ingredients in a food processor and mix until smooth. Place in an airtight container and freeze.

BOOK THREE

SAY GOODBYE TO THOSE STUBBORN BELLY FATS FOREVER

DIANA WATSON

TABLE OF CONTENTS

- THE MEGA GLUTEN-FREE COOKBOOK FOR THE SMART
- INTRODUCTION
- UNDERSTAND THE RESISTANCE
- INSULIN RESISTANCE DIET
- LONG-TERM MANAGEMENT
- DIET PLAN
- RECIPES
- INTRODUCTION
- THE PHASES
- MEAL PLAN
- RECIPES
- CONCLUSION

- **VIP Subscriber List**

- Hi Dear Reader, this is Diana! If you like my book and you want to receive the latest tips and tricks on cooking, weight-loss, cookbook recipes and more, do subscribe to my mailing list in the link below! I will then be able to send you the most up-to-date information about my upcoming books and promotions as well! Thank you for supporting my work and happy reading!

-

- **Subscriber Form**

    http://bit.do/dianawatson

INTRODUCTION

We have all tried to lose weight at some point in our lives. Some of us got lucky and found a diet that worked for us and that we liked. Others have stumbled through every diet out there, it seems like, and still can't lose the weight they're wanting to. The main reason that this type of dieting doesn't work is simple: simply going from one diet to another does not give our bodies a chance. And let's be honest here, we don't give the diets a chance either. Our bodies can't make the necessary adjustments in just a couple of days or even a week that it needs to make the weight loss happen. If one diet doesn't work for you, you really shouldn't just go running to another one. It isn't good for your body or your mind to do such a thing.

- There are so many different diets out there, and the majority of them are just fads that have not been proven to work. You are probably asking yourself "So what should I do now? Should I try low carb, high fat, all carbs, no carbs, no fat, low fat?"
- And indeed, most doctors and dietitians say the way to go is no fat. They say that fat is what makes you have a heart attack – that fat is your enemy. This, however, isn't entirely true.
- There are plenty of books on this subject on the market, thanks again for choosing this one! Every effort was made to ensure it is full of as much useful information as possible. Please enjoy!
-
-

-
- The fat that is burned will come from the stomach. This may not seem like it is crucial, but all fat is not equal. Everything depends on what area of the body the fat is found will determine what bad results it has on the body. There are two types of fat; visceral, which is stored in the stomach, and subcutaneous, which is stored under the skin. Visceral fat is the most dangerous because it is located around the organs. When there is too much fat in these areas, it will cause insulin resistance and inflammation. It is the main cause of metabolic dysfunction. Low carbs work great for lowering these harmful fats. This also drastically decreases the risk of getting type 2 Diabetes and heart disease.
- It will increase HDL levels. HDL is high-density lipoprotein. This is more popular known as good cholesterol. HDL and LDL

technically aren't cholesterol, but they are lipoproteins the hold onto the cholesterol and move it in the blood. HDL is great since it takes the cholesterol to the liver so that it can either be used or expelled. High levels of HDL will reduce your risk of heart disease. By eating more fats and fewer carbs will help to increase your HDL levels.

- Low carb can help to reduce insulin and blood sugar levels. Your system breaks down carbohydrates into simple sugars. These sugars will then make their way into your bloodstream and increases the levels of your blood sugar. The body then asks the insulin to fight these by choosing to either burn or store them. When people are healthy, insulin can do its job and prevents the sugars from hurting the healthy person. Some people have problems with insulin response. Insulin resistance is where the cells can't see the insulin, so this makes it hard for the body to take the blood sugar from the blood and into your cells. When the body can no longer secrete the correct amount of insulin, you run the risk of developing type 2 Diabetes. This affects around 300 million people. By reducing the intake of carbs, your body will no longer cause high blood sugar or insulin levels.

- **Good Foods**
- You might find it hard to figure out what you can eat. Here are some different types of foods that you are allowed to eat. For the record, all poultry, meat, and fish do not have carbs, so you are free to have as much as you want.
- Meats: you can eat any that you want as long as it isn't processed. This will include veal, venison, lamb, mutton, beef, and pork. You can eat both ham and bacon if they haven't been

processed.

- Poultry: You can eat all the poultry you want, such as turkey, chicken, goose, pheasant, duck, quail, Cornish hen, and ostrich. As long as the food is not processed, you are allowed to eat it.
- Seafood: Seafood is another food that you can eat as much of as you want. This will include herring, trout, sardines, snapper, salmon, tuna, and catfish. You can also have shellfish such as oysters, clams, shrimp, crab, calamari, mussels, scallops, and calamari. Never consume imitation crab meat. If you want crab meat, get the real stuff.
- Eggs are a fun food. You can have all the eggs fixed any way you would like them.
- Most vegetables are safe as well. There are some that you need to stay away from like corn, potatoes, peas, and any other starchy

vegetables. There are two different categories of vegetables which are salad and all others. The salad vegetables that you can eat are all lettuces, cucumber, all leafy herbs, bok choy, jicama, chives, olives, fennel, celery, mushrooms, parsley, sprouts, daikon, sweet and hot potatoes, and radishes.

- The other vegetables you can consume are asparagus, artichokes, cabbage, broccoli, cauliflower, leafy greens (mustard, turnip, beet, and collards), eggplant, Brussels sprouts, kale, avocado, tomatoes, okra, onions, summer squash, and zucchini.
- Try to consume oils that contain omega-3 fatty acids. Oils that are cold-pressed are the best. Fats that you can consume are olive oil, fat from meat, nut oils, butter (not margarine), seed oils, linseed oil, and vegetable oils.
- Most food becomes much better after adding

spices and condiments. Just because you are dieting, doesn't mean your food has to taste bad. Just watch out for store-bought condiments like salad dressing which are loaded with sugars. The best way to have salad dressings is to make them yourself. Read the ingredient label for carbs and subtract the dietary fiber/sugar alcohols to get net carbs if you're concerned about whether something is alright to eat. Whether making them at home or buying them at the store, here are some things that are fine for you to eat

- Condiments: sugar-free mayonnaise and ketchup, sugar-free and reduced sodium soy sauce.
- Spices: individual spices are fine. Just watch out for blends. They can have hidden sugars or maltodextrin.
- Salad dressings: best choice would be to make

your own using vinegar, lemon juice, and olive oil.

- Artificial sweeteners are fine to use. Never consume sugars like glucose, dextrose, maltose, fructose, and sucrose. Sugar alcohols like xylitol, sorbitol, and maltitol should never be consumed. Corn syrup and honey are off limits as well. The sweeteners that can be consumed are Equal (aspartame), Stevia, Splenda (sucralose), and Sweet 'n' Low (acesulfame potassium).
- Drinks: you need to drink eight 8 oz. glasses of water every day. This water should be tap, spring, mineral, or filtered. Try to stay away from caffeinated drinks. They can hurt blood sugars and appetite. These drinks are excellent to have: club soda, herbal tea (no fruit sugars or barley), flavored seltzers (needs to be zero calories), coffee, and tea.

- Alcohol: Consuming alcohol in beer, wine, or cocktails will risk slowing down the weight loss. Beer is nothing more than liquid bread since it is full of starch. You can have a glass of wine now and then during the second phase. You will need to check to see how many carbs are in each serving. A serving size is just 5 oz. so no huge wine glass full.

- Margarine: Margarine is an imitation butter, so it is not real food. It is very high in omega-6 fat. There are no health benefits. But it does have links to inflammatory disease, asthma, and allergies. Avoid margarine at all costs.

- Sauces: Most store-bought sauces have a lot of sugars in them. Check the label and look at the first ingredient to see if it is sugar. If it is, throw them out. Make your own so you can control the sugar.

- Sugar: This is the main thing to avoid. This

will include cereals, ice cream, pastries, buns, cakes, chocolate, sports drinks, juice, candy, and soft drinks. Sugars cause all kinds of problems with the body. Avoid them like the plague.

-
- THE PHASES
- This diet is broken down into four different phases the starts with the induction phase for two weeks. Then you will move into the second phase, balancing. Phase three is fine tuning. Phase four is maintenance.
-
- **Induction**
- This is the most restrictive phase of the diet. It only allows you to have 20 carbs every day. This equals about 3 cups of greens and non-starchy veggies. You will see the most weight loss during this phase. This gives you motivation for the future.
- You will need to stay in this phase until you are 15 pounds away from your goal weight. You will lose the unwanted weight a lot faster during this phase. This also gets your body to

stop burning carbs and starts burning fat.
- These foods must be avoided at all cost during this phase: alcohol, dairy (butter and cheese), starchy vegetables, grains, bread, fruit.
- You can consume these during phase one: club soda, bouillon, tea, coffee, water, non-starchy vegetables, eggs, cheese, meat, poultry, shellfish, and fish, etc.
- The important parts of induction are:
- Significant weight loss
- Lasts at least two weeks
- You can eat fatty condiments
- Only 20 carbohydrates every day
- Lots of protein; healthy fats, meats, eggs, poultry, and fish
- **Balancing**
- When you enter the next phase, you will begin to add whole food carbs slowly back into your diet. Foods like Greek yogurt, ricotta, heavy

cream, cottage cheese, walnuts, almonds, strawberries, melon, lemon, and tomato. You add them back in slowly until you find the right balance for you. This phase helps you maintain what you achieved during the first phase.

- You don't have a precise time frame for this phase. It has been suggested to stay on in this phase until you are about 10 pounds for your ideal weight. You can move to phase three whenever you want as long as you know that your weight loss will slow down.
- You will begin with 25 carbs a week and slowly increase them by 5 grams each week. You will gradually add healthy carbs back in until you find the right balance. This might be anywhere between 30 to 80 grams of carbs a day. Your gender, activity level and hormone status play important roles in this.

- This phase will help you find the right carb balance. It can also help you shed some excess weight. Phase one is the foundation diet. You will continue to eat foods that you could eat in phase one.
- Things to do in phase two are:
- Slowly introduce nutrient dense carbs back into the diet.
- Have your carbs back up to 25 carbs a day within a week.
- By week two have the carbs back up to 30 grams a day.
- You should continue to up your carb intake by 5 grams a week until you discover that the weight loss has stopped. Take the carb consumption down to a previous amount.
- **Fine-Tuning**
- By now you should be about 10 pounds away from your goal weight. This phase will help

you lose the rest of that weight and get to your goal. This is to fine-tune your diet so you can focus on keeping your ideal weight. This will show you how many carbs your body allows you to consume while maintaining your goal weight. You will stay in phase three until you get to your ideal weight, and can keep it off for one month.

- You start adding these foods back into your diet until you find the balance: oatmeal, peach, guava, cherries, apples, pinto beans, lima beans, chickpeas, yams, carrots, and other foods.
- This phase is there to help you shed those last few pounds and to test your carb balance. It will allow you to find your carb balance and help you to maintain your ideal weight.
- You increase your daily carb intake by 5 or 10-gram increments. Continue to introduce carbs

while still losing weight, and maintaining your weight loss.
- In this phase you will:
- Slowly increase carb intake by five to 10 grams a week until you are no longer losing weight, then drop it back down.
- Get to where you are losing less than a pound a week.
- **Maintenance**
- You have now entered the last phase of your diet. It shouldn't be thought of as the end of your diet but a beginning of your lifelong healthy lifestyle. You should know your carb balance by now. This will help you maintain your weight. You should be consuming about 75 net carbs each day. This is where you should stay.
- This will continue forever. This phase never ends.

- This is to help you find a permanent way to eat so that you can keep your weight at this goal.
- Your goal is to be able to maintain your weight by knowing how to adjust your carbohydrate intake as you need to. This means that you will know what to do if you ever need to gain or lose a few pounds.
- With this phase you will:
- Consume anywhere from 90 to 120 grams of carbs every day. This all depends on your activity level, age, and gender.
- Keep the same weight if you can keep your carb consumption the same as it was at the end of phase three.

-
-
-
-
-

-
- MEAL PLAN

- **Grocery List**

- 10 oz. pack frozen broccoli florets
- 1-lb sugar-free bacon
- 1-lb ground beef
- 10 oz. pack frozen spinach
- 1-lb ground turkey
- 1 rotisserie chicken, homemade or store-bought
- 12 oz. roll sugar-free breakfast sausage
- 1-lb package Italian pork sausage links
- 2.5 – 3-pound boneless chuck roast
- 8 oz. jar sugar-free salsa
- 1 can artichoke hearts packed in water
- Lite salt
- 2 bars Lindt 90 % chocolate
- 4 oz. can green chilies, chopped
- 1/2 -pound salted butter

- 8 oz. sliced pepper jack cheese
- 8 oz. string cheese
- 16 oz. heavy cream
- 8 oz. cream cheese
- ½ gallon almond milk, unsweetened
- 4 oz. feta cheese
- 3 dozen eggs
- 1 bunch basil
- 1 small head radicchio
- 1 large spaghetti squash
- 2 packages romaine lettuce hearts
- 8 oz. sour cream
- 2 heads cauliflower
- 2 tomatoes
- 16 oz. cheddar cheese
- 1 bunch celery
- 2 avocados
- 1 8 oz. bag baby spinach
- 2 red bell pepper

- **Prep**
- You might find that it is easier for you to prep everything on the weekend and then just reheat it as you go. Every one of these recipes reheats well. If you don't like prep work, just do a few at a time and make what you need as you go. It is up to you.
1. Bake the Cuban Pot Roast and divide it into portions to reheat through the week. Freeze anything that isn't used.
2. Make and bake the Sundried Tomato and Feta Meatballs. Any extras may be frozen. Try not to eat them all at one time.
3. Make the Antipasto Salad and split it into half cup portions. This should be consumed either room temp or cold.
4. Cook all of the bacon and keep in refrigerator until you need it. Reheat in microwave about 20 seconds before you eat.

5. Make the Cream Cheese Pancakes in two batches. Keep in refrigerator. You may need to heat it in the microwave for about 30 seconds to thin a bit.
6. Put together and bake the Chili Spaghetti Squash Casserole. Keep in refrigerator. Any extras should be frozen.
7. Fix the Easy Cauliflower Gratin and put in the refrigerator. Extras may be frozen.
8. Put together and bake the Spinach, Sausage and Feta Frittata. Slice it into squares that or four inches in size to have for the week. Keep in refrigerator. Extras can be frozen.
9. Remove meat from chicken. Place in airtight container and keep in the fridge. Place chicken carcass in a large stockpot with one gallon of water and peppercorns. Allow this to simmer for about 4 hours to create the chicken broth. Add water as it reduces down. There should

have between five and six cups of broth after the solids are strained out. Add lite salt at the end for your taste. Keep in refrigerator for the week or freeze.

10.
11. Seven-Day Meal Plan

12. **Day One**: 18g net carbs, 90g protein, 128g fat, 1609 calories

13. <u>Breakfast</u>: 8g net carbs, 33g fat, 14g protein, 384 calories

14. Coffee with 2 Tbsp. heavy cream

15. 2 pieces, cooked bacon

16. 2 cream cheese pancakes

17. <u>Snack</u>: 2g net carbs, 12g fat, 16g protein, 160 calories

18. 2 sticks of string cheese

19. <u>Lunch</u>: 458 calories, 40g fat, 27g protein, 6.5g net carbs

20. 4 sundried tomato & feta meatballs

21. ½ cup antipasto salad

22. <u>Snack</u>: 50 calories, 1g protein, 0g net carbs, 1g fat

23. 1 cup chicken broth

24. <u>Dinner</u>: 452 calories, 33g fat, 29g protein,

4.5g net carbs

25. ¼ cup cheddar cheese, shredded
26. 1 Tbsp. cilantro, chopped
27. 2 Tbsp. sour cream
28. 2 cups romaine lettuce, chopped
29. 1 cup Cuban pot roast
30. <u>Dessert</u>: 105 calories, 3g protein, 3g net carbs, 9g fat
31. 2 squares Lindt 90 percent Chocolate
32.
33. **Day Two**: 1604 calories, 122g fat, 89g protein, 19.5g net carbs
34. <u>Breakfast</u>: 463 calories, 37g fat, 25g protein, 8g net carbs
35. Coffee with 2 Tbsp. Heavy Cream
36. 2 pieces cooked bacon
37. 1 tsp butter
38. 3 eggs – fried or scrambled
39. <u>Snack</u>: 166 calories, 15g fat, 6g protein, 2g

net carbs

40. 24 raw almonds
41. Lunch: 452 calories, 33g fat, 29g protein, 4.5g net carbs
42. ¼ cup cheddar cheese, shredded
43. 1 Tbsp. cilantro, chopped
44. 2 Tbsp. sour cream
45. 2 cups romaine lettuce, chopped
46. 1 cup Cuban pot roast
47. Snack: 50 calories, 1g fat, 1g protein, 0g net carbs
48. 1 cup chicken broth
49. Dinner: 368 calories, 27g fat, 25g protein, 8g net carbs
50. 1 Tbsp. Sugar-free ranch dressing
51. 2 cups baby spinach, ran
52. 1 ½ cups Chili Spaghetti Squash Casserole
53. Dessert: 105 calories, 9g fat, 3g protein, 3g net carbs

54. 2 squares Lindt 90 percent Chocolate
55.
56. **Day Three**: 1649 calories, 132g fat, 81g protein, 18.5g net carbs
57. Breakfast: 384 calories, 33g fat, 14g protein, 2g net carbs
58. Coffee with 2 Tbsp. heavy cream
59. 2 pieces cooked bacon
60. 2 Cream Cheese Pancakes
61. Snack: 50 calories, 1g fat, 1g protein, 0g net carbs
62. 1 cup chicken broth
63. Lunch: 458 calories, 40g fat, 27g protein, 6.5g net carbs
64. 4 sundried tomato & feta meatballs
65. ½ cup antipasto salad
66. Snack: 200 calories, 16g fat, 7g protein, 2.5g net carbs
67. 5 stalks celery

68. 2 Tbsp. almond butter
69. <u>Dinner</u>: 452 calories, 33g fat, 29g protein, 4.5g net carbs
70. ¼ cup cheddar cheese, shredded
71. 1 Tbsp. cilantro, chopped
72. 1 Tbsp. sour cream
73. 2 cups romaine lettuce, chopped
74. 1 cup Cuban Pot Roast
75. <u>Dessert</u>: 105 calories, 9g fat, 3g protein, 3g net carbs
76. 2 squares Lindt 90 percent Chocolate
77.
78. **Day Four**: 1386 calories. 69g protein, 112g fat, 19.5g net carbs
79. <u>Breakfast</u>: 326 calories, 28g fat, 12g protein, 2g net carbs
80. Coffee with 2 Tbsp. heavy cream
81. 3-inch square Sausage & Spinach Frittata
82. <u>Snack</u>: 114 Calories, 11g fat, 1g protein, 1g

net carbs

83. ½ avocado w/lite salt and pepper
84. <u>Lunch:</u> 284 calories, 20g fat, 23g protein, 6g net carbs
85. 1 ½ cup Chili Spaghetti Squash Casserole
86. <u>Snack</u>: 50 calories, 1g fat, 1g protein, 0g net carbs
87. 1 cup chicken broth
88. <u>Dinner</u>: 507 calories, 43g fat, 29g protein, 7.5g net carbs
89. 1 Tbsp. Sugar-free Italian dressing
90. 2 cups baby spinach, raw
91. 4 Sundried tomato & feta meatballs
92. ½ cup antipasto
93. <u>Dessert</u>: 105 calories, 9g fat, 3g protein, 3g net carbs
94. 2 squares Lindt 90 percent chocolate
95.
96. **Day Five**: 1512 calories, 119g fat, 78g

protein, 18g net carbs

97. <u>Breakfast</u>: 384 calories, 33g fat, 14g protein, 2[g net carbs

98. Coffee with 2 Tbsp. heavy cream

99. 2 pieces cooked bacon

100. 2 cream cheese pancakes

101. Snack: 160 calories, 12g fat, 16g protein, 2g net carbs

102. 2 sticks string cheese

103. <u>Lunch</u>: 445 calories, 37g fat, 19g protein, 3g net carbs

104. ¾ cup easy cauliflower gratin

105. 1 Italian sausage link, sliced and cooked

106. <u>Snack</u>: 50 calories, 1g fat, 1g protein, 0g net carbs

107. 1 cup chicken broth

108. <u>Dinner</u>: 368 calories, 27g fat, 25g protein, 8g net carbs

109. 1 Tbsp. Sugar-free ranch dressing

110. 2 cups baby spinach, raw
111. 1 ½ cup chili spaghetti squash casserole
112. Dessert: 105 calories, 9g fat, 3g protein, 3g net carbs
113. 2 squares Lindt 90 percent chocolate
114.
115. **Day Six**: 1636 calories, 88g protein, 126g fat, 18.5g net carbs
116. Breakfast: 326 calories, 28g fat, 12g protein, 2g net carbs
117. Coffee with 2 Tbsp. heavy cream
118. 3-inch square sausage & spinach frittata
119. Snack: 200 calories, 16g fat, 7g protein, 2.5g net carbs
120. 5 stalks celery
121. 2 Tbsp. almond butter
122. Lunch: 462 calories, 29g fat, 44g protein, 3g. net carbs
123. 1 cup leftover chicken, chopped

124. 2 Tbsp. Sugar-free Caesar salad dressing
125. 2 cup romaine lettuce, chopped
126. Snack: 114 calories, 11g fat, 1g protein, 1g net carbs
127. ½ avocado w/ pepper and lite salt
128. Dinner: 429 calories, 33g fat, 21g protein, 7g net carbs
129. 2 Tbsp. parmesan cheese, grated
130. 1 Tbsp. butter
131. 1 cup broccoli, cooked
132. 1 Italian sausage link., sliced and cooked
133. Dessert: 105 calories, 9g fat, 3g protein, 3g net carbs
134. 2 squares Lindt 90 percent chocolate
135.
136. **Day Seven**: 1650 calories, 88g protein, 132g fat, 14g net carbs
137. Breakfast: 326 calories, 28g fat, 12g protein, 2g net carbs

138. Coffee with 2 Tbsp. heavy cream

139. 3-inch square sausage & spinach frittata

140. <u>Snack</u>: 114 calories, 11g fat, 1g protein, 1g net carbs

141. ½ avocado w/pepper and salt

142. <u>Lunch</u>: 262 calories, 21g fat, 16g protein, 1g net carbs

143. 2 slices cooked bacon

144. 2 Romaine lettuce leaves

145. ½ cup simple egg salad

146. <u>Snack</u>: 166 calories, 15g fat, 6g protein, 2g net carbs

147. 24 raw almonds

148. <u>Dinner</u>: 677 calories, 48g fat, 50g protein, 5g net carbs

149. 2 Tbsp. Sugar-free Caesar salad dressing

150. 2 cups romaine lettuce, chopped

151. ¾ cup easy cauliflower gratin

152. 6 oz. rotisserie chicken

153. <u>Dessert</u>: 105 calories, 9g fat, 3g protein, 3g net carbs

154. 2 squares Lindt 90 percent chocolate

155. RECIPES

156. Sides, Snacks, and Extras

157. Cauliflower Gratin

158. Ingredients

- Salt
- 4 Tbsp. butter
- Pepper
- 1/3 cup heavy whipping cream
- 6 slices pepper jack cheese
- 4 cups cauliflower florets
- Directions
- Grab a microwave-safe bowl and in it, combine cauliflower, pepper, salt, cream, and butter. Microwave on high about 25 minutes until soft enough to mash with a fork. Keep in mind that all microwaves work differently. I recommend

starting with ten minutes, check it and continue in five-minute increments until fork tender.

- Once tender, mash with potato masher or fork. Taste and adjust seasonings if needed. Put cheese slices on top and microwave another couple of minutes until cheese is melted.
- Serve piping hot.
-

-
- Ranch Dressing
- Ingredients
- ¼ tsp pepper
- 2 tsp lemon juice
- 2 tsp Dijon mustard
- ¾ cup mayonnaise
- ½ cup heavy cream
- ½ tsp salt
- 1 tsp fresh dill
- 2 Tbsp. Parsley
- ½ tsp garlic
- 2 Tbsp. Chopped chives
- Directions
- Mix everything in a bowl until smooth.
- Use immediately or place in airtight container and refrigerate for up to 3 days.
-
- Coconut Almond Minute Muffin

- Ingredients
- 1 tsp olive oil
- 1 large egg
- ¼ tsp baking powder
- 1/8 tsp salt
- 2 Tbsp. Almond flour
- 1 tsp sweetener
- ½ tsp cinnamon
- 1/3 Tbsp. coconut flour
- Directions
- Put all dry ingredients in a microwave safe coffee mug. Stir to combine.
- Add oil and egg. Stir until thoroughly combined.
- Microwave 1 minute. Use a knife to help remove from cup, slice, butter, eat.
-
-

-
- **Breakfast**
- Spinach, Sausage and Feta Frittata
- Ingredients
- ¼ tsp ground nutmeg
- 12 oz. mild sausage
- ¼ tsp black pepper
- 10 oz. spinach (thawed and drained if frozen)
- ½ tsp salt
- ½ cup almond milk, unsweetened
- 12 eggs
- ½ cup heavy cream
- ½ cup feta, crumbled
- Directions
- Your oven should be at 375.
- Break up raw sausage into crumbles and place in a bowl. Squeeze all liquid from spinach and put in a bowl with sausage. Sprinkle with feta cheese and toss to combine. Place mixture in

bottom of 13 x 9 casserole dish that has been greased.
- In a large bowl, combine eggs, nutmeg, pepper, salt, and almond milk. Whisk until thoroughly combined. Pour into casserole dish over the sausage mixture.
- Bake for 50 minutes until firmly set. Serve either room temperature or warm.
-

- Cream Cheese Pancakes
- Ingredients
- ½ tsp cinnamon
- 2 oz. cream cheese
- 1 tsp. sweetener
- 2 eggs
- Directions
- Put everything in your blender and mix until it is all smooth. Rest for a couple of minutes to let bubbles settle.

- Pour ¼ batter onto a hot griddle that has been sprayed with Pam. Cook two minutes until golden and bubbly. Flip and continue to cook for another minute. Repeat until no more batter.
- Serve with syrup of choice and fresh berries.
- **Lunch**
- Simple Egg Salad
- Ingredients
- Salt
- Pepper
- 6 eggs
- 1 tsp lemon juice
- 2 Tbsp. mayonnaise
- 1tsp Dijon mustard
- Directions
- Put eggs in saucepan filled with cold water. Boil for ten minutes.
- Take off heat and run under cold water. Peel

eggs under cool running water.
- Place eggs in food processor. Pulse until chopped. Add mayonnaise, pepper, salt, lemon juice, and mustard.
- Serve with lettuce leaves and bacon if desired.
-
- Antipasto Salad
- Ingredients
- Salt
- Pepper
- 2 cups finely chopped cauliflower
- 3 Tbsp. olive oil
- ½ cup chopped radicchio
- 3 Tbsp. balsamic vinegar
- ½ cup chopped artichoke hearts
- 1 clove minced garlic
- 1/3 cup chopped basil
- 3 Tbsp. chopped Kalamata olives
- ½ cup grated parmesan

- 3 Tbsp. chopped sundried tomatoes
- Directions
- Cook the cauliflower for five minutes in the microwave on a microwavable plate. You are not adding any liquid or seasonings now. Let cool.
- Toss together radicchio, garlic, olives, sundried tomatoes, parmesan, basil, and artichoke hearts in a bowl.
- Afterward, whisk vinegar and oil together. Pour over salad. Toss to mix. Season with pepper and salt.
- Serve either cold or room temperature.
-

- Feta and Sun-dried Tomato Meatballs
- Ingredients
- 2 Tbsp. water
- 1 lb. ground turkey
- ½ cup almond flour

- ¼ cup crumbled feta
- ½ tsp garlic powder
- 2 Tbsp. Chopped sundried tomatoes
- 1 egg
- 1 Tbsp. Chopped thyme
- Directions
- Mix everything in a bowl. Form 16 meatballs.
- Warm oil in sauté pan. Cook meatballs in sauté pan for about three to four minutes per side until crispy and browned. Don't crowd the pan or they won't cook properly.
- When done, take out of pan and place on paper towels to drain. You can eat these by themselves or with marinara sauce and spaghetti squash to make a complete meal.
-

-

- **Dinner**

- Cuban Pot Roast
- Ingredients
- 2 Tbsp. apple cider vinegar
- 2.5 – 3-pound chuck roast, boneless
- ½ tsp black pepper
- ½ cup salsa verde
- 1 Tbsp. ground coriander
- 1 can chop green chilies
- 1 Tbsp. chili powder
- 1 tsp oregano
- 1 tsp garlic powder
- 1 cup diced tomatoes
- ½ cup red bell pepper, sliced into strips
- 2 Tbsp. dehydrated onion
- 2 Tbsp. cumin
- 1 tsp salt
- Directions

- Season roast with pepper and salt well. Heat skillet and sear roast on all sides until browned.
- Put in a slow cooker. Add tomatoes, chilies, and salsa verde in the skillet. Deglaze skillet and bring mixture to boil. Take off heat. Add apple cider vinegar, pepper, chili powder, oregano, coriander, cumin, salt, bell pepper, garlic, and onion flakes. Mix well.
- Pour over meat. Set on low and cook for six hours. Shred meat. Serve with toppings of choice.
-

- Chili Spaghetti Squash Casserole
- Ingredients
- For Chili:
- Salt
- 1tsp oregano
- Pepper

- 1 lb. lean ground beef
- ½ cup prepared salsa
- 1 tsp coriander
- ½ tsp garlic powder
- 1 tsp ground cumin
- 1 Tbsp. chipotles in adobo, chopped
- For Casserole:
- 1 ¾ cup Mexican cheese, shredded
- 4 cups cooked spaghetti squash
- ¾ cup sour cream
- 2 Tbsp. melted butter
- Toppings:
- Avocado
- Salsa
- Sour cream
- Cilantro, chopped
- Directions:
- For Chili:
- Brown ground beef in a skillet. Add pepper

and salt to meat. Drain fat. Add rest of chili ingredients. Bring chili mixture to a boil, then simmer mixture for 10 minutes.

- For Casserole:
- Mix spaghetti squash and butter. Toss to coat. Season with pepper and salt.
- Put into 14-inch casserole dish. Sprinkle with ¾ cup cheese. Spread with sour cream. Add chili on to and spread out in an even layer. Leave about an inch around the edge. Place the rest of the cheese on top. Oven should be at 350. Cook 30 minutes
- Serve warm with topping of choice.

-
- **Dessert**
- Banana Split Cake
- Ingredients
- For Crust:
- 1 cup melted butter
- 1/3 cup sweetener
- 2 tsp cinnamon
- 3 cups almond flour
- For Filling:
- 1 cup melted butter
- 1 cup artificial powdered sugar
- 16 oz. cream cheese
- For Topping:
- 3 Tbsp. sweetener
- 3 Tbsp. water
- 1 tsp vanilla extract
- 1 ½ tsp gelatin
- 2 cups heavy whipping cream

- 1 Tbsp. lemon juice
- 1 chopped banana
- 2 pints sliced strawberries
- Optional Toppings:
- Chocolate sauce
- Chopped nuts
- Directions
- Place all crust ingredients into a 13 x 9-inch pan. Mix well and press into an even layer.
- Mix butter, confectioner's sweetener, and cream cheese until smooth.
- Spread evenly on top of the crust.
- Mix bananas and strawberries in a bowl with lemon juice.
- Layer this over the cream cheese. Spread evenly.
- Make the whipped cream by softening the gelatin in water. Add this to mixing bowl with heavy cream and vanilla. Beat until stiff peaks

form. Spoon over top of strawberries and bananas and spread evenly.
- Top with chocolate sauce and chopped nuts.
-
- Death by Chocolate Cheesecake
- Ingredients
- For Crust:
- 3 Tbsp. melted butter
- 1 ¼ cup almond flour
- ¼ cup sweetener
- ¼ cup cocoa powder
- For Filling:
- 2 tsp melted butter for brushing pan
- 6 oz. chopped sugar-free dark chocolate
- 1/3 cup room temperature heavy cream
- 1 Tbsp. butter
- ¼ cup cocoa powder
- 24 oz. softened cream cheese
- 3 large room temperature eggs

- ½ cup sweetener
- 1 tsp vanilla extract
- ½ cup powdered sweetener
- For Topping:
- ½ tsp vanilla extract
- ¾ cup whipping cream
- 3 oz. finely chopped unsweetened chocolate
- 1/3 cup artificial confectioner's sweetener
- Directions
- Crust:
- The oven should be at 325. Whisk together sweetener, cocoa powder, and almond flour. Add butter, stir until well combined.
- Press the crust into a springform pan. Cook for 10 – 12 minutes. Take out of the oven and reduce temp to 300.
- Filling:
- On the stove top, melt butter and chocolate in a pan, stir until smooth. Let cool.

- Mix the cream cheese until smooth. Mix in vanilla and sweeteners. Add eggs each one by one. Make sure eggs are in; scrape down sides of bowl if you need to.
- Add heavy cream and cocoa powder until combined. Add melted chocolate until smooth.
- Brush springform pan with melted butter. Don't touch the crust. Pour filling into pan and shake to even out. Bake 55 to 60 minutes. The filling should be set but jiggly in the center.
- Take out of the oven and allow to cool 15 minutes. Slide a sharp knife around the sides. Cool completely. When cooled completely, remove spring form pan. Cover with plastic wrap tightly and place in refrigerator for 3 hours.
- Topping:
- Combine sweetener and cream in pan. Bring to simmer and take off heat. Add vanilla and

chopped chocolate. Let sit for five minutes and whisk until smooth.
- Pour over cheesecake. Allow to drip down sides. Chill until set.

-

-

-

- The next step is to take all these tips and tricks and learn how to eat a low-carb and high-fat diet to melt that weight right off.

-
-
-
-
-
-
-
-
-